WHY I BROKE UP WITH MY COMPANY

PRAISE FOR
WHY I BROKE UP WITH MY COMPANY

"Marissa so eloquently captures and expresses the essence of what many of us experience — the ups and downs with any relationship. *Why I Broke Up with My Company* provides a raw and honest look into the depths of relationships built within corporate structures, and the difficult decisions one must make every now and then to allow the relationship to grow (whether together or apart). Her guiding message — embrace authentic support (your "Personal Board of Directors") and take control — is sound advice for all!"

Laurie Miller

CIO and Head of IT, Covestro Deutschland AG

"This book serves as an important reminder to beware of the pitfalls of career complacency. *Why I Broke Up with My Company* makes clear that while it's easy to get caught up in the honeymoon phase of any job, at the end of the day, *you* own your career. If you don't take control over your career, someone else will. And even though breaking up with a job can be difficult but necessary for your career and sanity, you don't have to do it alone! A trusted group of mentors, or as Marissa Lee brilliantly calls them, a "board of directors," can guide and advise you through your career development. Get this book now if you want to take ownership of your career!"

Eric L. Williamson

Speaker and Author of *How to Work with Jerks: Getting Stuff Done with People You Can't Stand*

"It is a great joy for an educator when a former student evolves in her career and finds satisfaction in personal and career growth! Marissa Lee was my former Human Resources Management student at The Ohio State University. She was inquisitive then, and always probing for growth opportunities when she entered the workforce as a young professional. The description of her very personal journey and her resulting evolution — as described in this well-written book — offers tools to enhance performance wherever you are in your career. Definitely a must-read."

Nancy K. Lahmers, JD
Retired Faculty, The Ohio State University

"Marissa invites readers along for a vivid recap of her career journey by candidly sharing the ups and downs of self-discovery, mindset shifting, and accountability.

She brought back so many memories from a time when I left a long-time position in nonprofit recruiting in hopes of growth — only to end up back on the market shortly thereafter. Much like Marissa, I found that this experience forced me to get real with myself and dig deep into what was most important, so I could obtain the career destined for me.

This book is a must-read for anyone who's feeling the itch to step out on faith and land a job they love. Be prepared to take deep dives into your goals and tap into your network of supporters because, although it may be a wild ride, your future self will thank you for not accepting anything less than the right-fit role (or company) you deserve."

Ashley Watkins, NCRW
Career Coach and Certified Résumé Writer, Write Step Résumés, LLC

"Personal and professional growth come when an individual will take an honest look at their journey so they might learn and adjust. While Marissa's book hinges on a journey that is specific to her, readers who are considering the reflective pause of a 'stay or go' decision will surely garner some insight from her perspectives and advice."

David R. Baumgartner, SPHR, SHRM-SCP, SSGB, CNA
Author, Coach, Workplace Balance Expert, and
VP of Spirituality at Signature Healthcare

"We often spend time dreaming about the end goal of our careers, rather than how to navigate the ups and downs along the journey. Marissa's conversational approach pushes employees to thoughtfully take ownership of their careers, exploring options early and often. I love the tools throughout the book, including letters to employers and ways you can E.V.O.L.V.E. This book has the ability to impact careers across generations."

Ann Brown, SPHR, MS HRD
Vice President of Talent Management at German American,
Founder & CEO of The Development Edge, and Author of
You@Work: Unlocking Human Potential in the Workplace

"Marissa Lee's book is an important reminder that we must each take responsibility for our own lives, careers, and happiness. Her step-by-step guide to thriving professionally, regardless of the ups and downs of any employment relationship, is useful for anyone trying to navigate the career lattice of corporate America."

Amy C. Waninger
CEO of Lead at Any Level and author of *Network Beyond Bias*

"Owning your life may challenge you to contemplate your mindset, evaluate your relationships, and take the lead in seeking your successes. But many overlook the fact that career ownership has the power to impact *all* aspects of your life. *Why I Broke Up with My Company* challenges you to dig deep within, questioning how your career trajectory can help you fulfill your life's purpose. A must-read for those newly jumping into the career force, for those who are wavering in their career decisions, and for those who need the affirmation that they, indeed, own their lives and their career choices."

Stephanie Feger

Author of *Color Today Pretty: An Inspirational Guide to Living a Life in Perspective*

"This book is a must-have for so many reasons. As I travel all over the world, talking about how to attract and retain employees in today's workforce, it's clear that this book solves the problems. It is all about relationships! Many organizations focus on the different generations, communication, and technology -- which are important -- but forget we are relational human beings. In her book, Marissa Lee provides some clear and relevant insight into today's workforce by tackling some relevant challenges from a relationship standpoint."

Tonia Morris

Global Transition Coach, Millennial & Generational Connection Speaker, Author, and Founder of Simply HR, LLC

WHY I BROKE UP WITH MY COMPANY

WITH MY COMPANY

Lessons in Career Ownership

MARISSA LEE

SILVER TREE
PUBLISHING

Why I Broke Up with My Company: Lessons in Career Ownership

Copyright 2019 by Marissa Lee

Published by Silver Tree Publishing, a division of
Silver Tree Communications, LLC (Kenosha, WI).
www.SilverTreePublishing.com

Some company names and names of individuals have been changed
throughout to protect privacy.

Editing by:
Courtney Hudson

Cover design and typesetting by:
Courtney Hudson

First edition, July 2019

ISBN: 978-1-948238-12-0

Library of Congress Control Number: 2019937401

Created in the United States of America

DEDICATION

To my God, thanks for allowing me to increase in favor.

To my family, thanks for living this story with me and encouraging me along the way.

To my Gram, Juanita Melker Williams, though you have gone home to glory, thanks for always taking my side. Love you always.

To my HR-ettes and our Road Manager, Mama Bear, thanks for being my professional muses and personal ears.

> **For I know the thoughts that I think toward you, saith the Lord, thoughts of peace, and not of evil, to give you an expected end.**
>
> *– Jeremiah 29:11*

TABLE OF CONTENTS

FOREWORD

A NOTE FOR EMPLOYERS
WHO NEED TO RETAIN TALENT

Many years ago, my grandfather worked on the line at a Colgate factory. I've often wondered whether he enjoyed his career there but, the truth is, that element didn't matter back then. He was the sole breadwinner for a family of five and he had a pension. It likely never crossed his mind to consider going elsewhere, because he had a stable paycheck that would provide for his family, and that was the primary contribution of a father and husband in those days.

However, the employer/employee relationship is much different today, and now offers no financial promises or guarantees of longevity. Even if companies offer pensions, their newest workers don't believe they will ever see those long-term benefits come to fruition. Because of this shift, the new employer/employee relationship relies on being mutually beneficial, or one side will abandon ship. So long as everyone is benefitting, the relationship can stay intact. But if an organization needs to restructure to remain competitive, layoffs will occur. And if new hires' needs aren't being met, they will find a better fit elsewhere.

In addition to this relationship change, during the past decade, the employment market and workforce have also changed dramatically.

Today, we are in an employee's market, where staff and applicants have the upper hand because nearly every business is hiring and applicants have more employment options. That means organizations that want to remain profitable and sustainable must continue to evolve over time, and yet many leaders are still managing people the same way they did 20 years ago — in the late 1900s. (The book you hold in your hands right now has a great deal to say about how individuals and organizations can do just that: E.V.O.L.V.E.)

As a retention expert who works with companies to reduce unnecessary employee turnover, I explain these dynamics and work to build better leaders for our client companies. In some situations, it's heartbreaking for me to see negative individuals singlehandedly destroy what could be a prize place of employment — an organization where leaders and managers are beginning to understand the situation and work tirelessly to create a culture where people WANT to work. *This isn't happening within your organization, is it?* Have you witnessed people being promoted into management and supervisory roles who were either not the right person for the job in the first place or perhaps they were never given the tools, time, and training to be effective in those positions?

Employers, if you take an honest look at your organizational culture and your own approach as a leader, have you and the company evolved to meet the needs and wishes of your new internal customers (i.e., your employees) as you have likely already done for your external customers? Or is it time to reevaluate "the way it's always been done" by listening and watching as differences appear in our workforce? Are you making the necessary adjustments to become a more effective leader, or do you plan to continue passing along the deeply engrained expectations that *you* were taught to the next generation of workers?

As you read Marissa Lee's book, put yourself in your employees' shoes and consider how your team members would answer her powerful questions as they make their decisions to stay or go. *Would you want to work for you?*

And employees, you don't owe anyone anything. But it's important to look ahead as to what you want your career path to look like when you gaze back upon it 20 years from now. Will you have wished you stayed put longer and weathered some of the storms? Or will you have been regretful of sacrificing so much for little in return? This book is going to help you make the best decision possible at this stage, and likely again at another point in your life.

The workforce has evolved and, as changes continue, it's time for leaders and employees to decide what they want the employer/employee relationship to look like moving forward. Marissa's book can help.

Cara Silletto, MBA

Workforce thought leader and keynote speaker, Cara Silletto, MBA, is the author of Staying Power: Why Your Employees Leave & How to Keep Them Longer. *Cara and her retention team at Crescendo Strategies work with clients across the country to reduce unnecessary employee turnover by making leaders more effective in their roles and helping organizations create a place where people WANT to work.*

INTRODUCTION

LETTER FROM THE AUTHOR

We almost made it to a milestone anniversary. For more than a year, I'd known that the honeymoon was over and that we weren't going to make it, yet I still hung on. I wasn't ready to leave. We had many ups and downs, which is normal in any relationship. But the downs started to supersede the good times. It was then that I realized it was finally "that" time. It was the time I'd been dreading; the time I knew would be bittersweet. It was finally time to break up with my company.

The decision didn't come easy, but it was necessary. It allowed me to leave on amicable terms, and also to look fondly back on the many good memories I did have with the company. I don't regret my decision, though I had no idea at the time that I would find myself facing similar crossroads only a short two years later. I had no idea I was about to enter a toxic situation that threatened my peace, my spirit, and my personal brand. Even still, these challenges gave me a chance to learn more about what I wanted for myself, and helped me to find a situation that was better for both my personal and career growth.

Though my journey is unique to me, I'm sure many people can relate to my experience. Many will come to that crossroads in their own career where they will wonder if it's time to move on.

By telling my story, I hope to spark a healthy dialogue about career development and ownership. It is my hope that you will walk away from this book with useful tools to help you navigate your own career development, and to help you E.V.O.L.V.E. into your greatest self by Evaluating, Vocalizing, Owning, Liberating, Validating, and Elevating your efforts.

1

THERE IS BLISS BEFORE THE STORM

Most personal relationships start out on a good note. In the beginning, you are in the getting-to-know-you phase, where you see things through an optimistic lens. Both of you are happy and you find yourself smiling all the time for no apparent reason. You are living in a bubble called bliss. You aren't thinking about the challenges you may face in the future — the storms that are sure to arise — but it's still important that you prepare for those moments if you want to ensure that your relationship remains strong. The same goes for your professional relationships and career.

When you start a new job, you are wooed by the novelty of the situation. Let's face it — you have yet to learn the things that annoy you about your employer. You have yet to be impacted by decisions you don't agree with, nor have you yet been sucked into the cesspool of negativity that these decisions can sometimes create. Your focus is on your new job and making a positive impact, which is a great mindset to have.

I know what you're probably thinking: "If everything is going well, why should I be thinking about what's next?" To that, I'd ask you, "Why not?" You should always be **evaluating** your career. People often fail to think about the future until it's too late, until their decisions have become clouded by emotions. Don't let things get to that point. You should always give some thought to your professional future and prepare for your next steps.

> I know what you're probably thinking: "If everything is going well, why should I be thinking about what's next?" To that, I'd ask you, "Why not?"

The E.V.O.L.V.E. Model
Step 1 – Evaluate

In publishing this book, I am calling readers to take action — in their lives and in their careers. It is my hope that *Why I Broke Up with My Company* provides individuals and organizations with inspiration to help them evaluate, vocalize, own, liberate, validate and elevate (E.V.O.L.V.E.) in career ownership. Throughout this book, I've provided sidebars on each step of the E.V.O.L.V.E. process, to help you further apply the book's stories and lessons by giving you a memorable framework that you can customize and apply to your own unique situation. Let's start by focusing on the evaluation process, looking first at its dictionary definition (Merriam-Webster).

Evaluate: (verb) to determine the significance, worth, or condition of something by careful appraisal and study

This doesn't mean becoming an opportunist. We all know that person who's better at schmoozing than working, or who hasn't been in a role long enough to accomplish anything because they are always looking for the next chance to move up. Don't be *that* person; no one likes an opportunist. Instead, what I'm suggesting is that you embrace another "O" word — ownership. You need to own your career.

> **No one likes an opportunist. Instead, what I'm suggesting is that you embrace another "O" word — ownership. You need to own your career.**

Evaluation is a critical part of owning your career. It's essential in determining appropriate career opportunities, identifying the skills/competencies needed to be successful, recognizing the best working environment and the people you have around you, and a plethora of other things that will be necessary for your career journey. Because it can sometimes be challenging to effectively evaluate ourselves, having key people who can help you with this process is critical. This group of people is your personal Board of Directors.

Who are your personal Board of Directors? As you evaluate who may either already be a part of your personal Board of Directors or those you may want to include moving forward, keep in mind that if you have the right people and network around you, your vision is set up to succeed. Your network will help you identify and fulfill your purpose.

You should have a vision of where you want to take your career, what skills you need to acquire, what competencies you need to develop, what relationships you need to build, how to achieve the highest level of performance, etc. It's up to you to navigate through the peaks and valleys. It's up to you to plan for the sunshine and the storms. You have to be in tune with how you want your career to progress and grow.

When you think about career growth, I propose looking at the *quality* of progression instead of the speed. When people focus on quality, they usually learn more and are ultimately more satisfied with the pace of their career growth (i.e., by not focusing on speed/pace, quality ends up driving the right/optimal pace). Doing so can also make people more open to different growth opportunities, including those outside the traditional career ladder.

Many people who focus strictly on time (e.g., on how fast they are considered for the next promotion, etc.) will rush their progress, and often can fail to explore other career opportunities that may not fit their predetermined timeline. Don't let an artificial obsession with time keep you from reaching your full potential. Embrace the organic evolution of your career; understand your value and how that can translate to new opportunities.

> **Don't let an artificial obsession with time keep you from reaching your full potential.**

This is why I avidly support having continuous development dialogues with your supervisor. I have found this approach helps keep people more open-minded in regard to their career development and paths. This can also give business and HR leaders a greater ability to support and assist their employees in advancing their individual career aspirations.

....

DEAR EMPLOYER,

You play an essential role in creating a culture that provides employees with experiences and a line of sight to developmental opportunities. It is important to create a culture where it's safe to make mistakes in order to give your employees the freedom to learn and be innovative. Whether you're talking about their Love Language or Myers-Briggs Type, individuals have unique perspectives of the world, and preferences about how they like to be engaged. Evaluation is critical to shifting the culture. As you review your culture, it is important to first understand your current culture. Then you should take some time to identify the characteristics of your aspirational culture. Once this process is complete, it is important to do a gap analysis to fully understand what is necessary to shift the culture. Then you need to assess the organization's readiness/maturity to support the change.

The same could be said about your employee engagement strategy, as it needs to be built on a strong culture. It's vital to have a strong sense of your talent, their development needs, and how you can support them. In an effort to match your employees' growth with your talent development portfolio, running an organizational diagnostic is as critical as hiring the right people. A one-size-fits-all approach does not effectively maximize employee engagement — customization is key. Everyone wants to feel special. Everyone wants to feel valued, whether it's your top talent or your consistent performer.

....

So let's talk about business and HR leaders for a second. If you're the driver of your career (a "pilot" or "captain," metaphorically speaking), then your supervisor and HR leader are co-pilots who will provide you with different career paths, such as becoming a subject-matter expert or people leader. Don't let them sleep through the whole trip, and don't be afraid to ask for help if you get "lost." It's important to get them involved early in the process and to maintain a continuous conversation about your career growth. You have to leverage these connections. This also goes for your network as a whole; building relationships is a critical part of your career. There's some truth to the sayings "It's not *what* you know but *who* you know," and "You're only as strong as your network." No one gets to where they are going if they go it alone. Your network will play many roles in your journey, whether it's because of the experience someone pours into you, or refining your key competencies as you pour your own experience into others.

⋮ **It's not *what* you know but *who* you know.**

The trusted members of my network definitely played big roles in my decision to leave different companies. No one ever told me outright to quit, but they did share their experiences, dropped many golden nuggets of wisdom, offered a listening ear, and supported me through the good and bad times.

These relationships formed organically, but I was definitely intentional with my engagement. It was important to me that my interactions be genuine, which ensured that my relationships developed on an unpretentious foundation. If you are looking to gain a mentor or grow your network, I suggest starting with a sincere interest and firm understanding of topics on which you'd like guidance (e.g., a mentor's career journey, a challenge you are dealing with that connects with the mentor's expertise, etc.). Then see how the relationship blossoms. There is no limit to the number of mentors and advisors you can have, but it is important to understand what role each of these people plays in your network and career development.

Recently someone asked me, "Who is on your personal Board of Directors?" The question made me reflect on my network and who helps me oversee my career and brand.

DEAR EMPLOYEE,

Now I'm going to ask you, "Who's on your personal Board of Directors?" As you evaluate your personal Board of Directors and your network in general, it's important to understand whether you have the right people around you and the right access to people who can support your vision. Your network will help you identify and/or fulfill your purpose, or not ... so choose wisely.

Personal Board of Directors Selection Criteria

Identify individuals:

- *With your best interests at heart (i.e., people who want to see you win)*

- *Who always tell you the truth no matter the situation (i.e., people who will challenge you)*

- *Who can provide you different perspectives (e.g., people outside your industry, function, etc.)*

- *Who can connect you with people outside of your current network (e.g., a sponsor)*

- *Who inspire you (i.e., people who are successful in their own right or bring out the best in you)*

2

ROCKY TIMES, HARD WAVES

I started my career wide-eyed and full of glee. I was so excited about the opportunities before me. There were no bells. There were no whistles. They didn't roll out the red carpet, but I didn't care. I was happy with my company-embroidered notebook and pen and was ready to be great.

I didn't expect much and didn't ask for more because I had this misguided notion that I needed to come in, prove myself, and everything would work out on its own. I didn't **vocalize** my career aspirations or compensation expectations. I thought that my company would take care of me. However, as I reflect on my part in this failed working relationship, I realized if I didn't communicate my wants and needs, how could I hold them fully responsible for knowing those details? This helped me learn, early on, not to leave things up to chance — that I must vocalize what I want in my career and speak up if my contributions weren't being appropriately valued. At that time, I didn't leverage all of the things I was bringing to the table, and I didn't require that my employer handle me like a talent from the start. This unfortunately set the wrong tone out of the gate, and that's a mistake I have to own. It was also a mistake that laid the groundwork for some of the challenges I would face.

At some of my previous employers, I started having doubts about my longevity long before I made the decisions to move on. I wasn't happy and I would find myself becoming more critical of the companies' decisions and their lack of follow-through on commitments. I started dreading coming to work. I know I shared these feelings with some of my colleagues, many of whom stayed and disregarded the signs that they had reached their own breaking points. I realized I had over-stayed my welcome because ...

... EVERYTHING HAD BECOME ROUTINE

Routine can be one of the biggest enemies of engagement. As people grow comfortable in their roles and things become repetitive, they often develop a strong desire for something new. This is why healthy, long-lasting personal relationships need to maintain some level of spice and spontaneity, and a job is no different. When you start feeling like your job is monotonous and stagnant, that's an early indication it's time for a change. Once you understand why you are feeling this way, you can determine if you need to explore other opportunities within the organization, or whether it's time to move on.

> When you start feeling like your job is monotonous and stagnant, that's an early indication it's time for a change.

In a typical personal relationship, you often have friends to confide in when you need to talk through your feelings. In the workplace, you can often find special colleagues, perhaps members of your personal Board of Directors, who can serve in this capacity as well. When

I was processing my feelings on moving forward, I happened to share with a colleague that I felt disenchanted with HR. He followed up by asking, "Are you disenchanted with HR or are you disenchanted with HR *here*?" That really made me think a little deeper about why I was feeling the way I was. I had to peel back a few layers to honestly answer the question, and discovered that there were different emotions I needed to process. I realized I was ...

... FEELING UNAPPRECIATED

In a personal relationship, it's not usually the big things, but the little things that are often overlooked. It's the "thanks for ..." or the "I liked when you did ..." that makes the difference. The same goes for the workplace. It's not always about money. Yes, people want to make sure they get paid what they are "worth," but, intuitively, we all know that equation doesn't often balance with our expectations. But there is something leaders can leverage that doesn't cost anything, and that's recognition of their teams' work. "Atta' Boys or Girls" can go a long way in reinforcing employees' satisfaction in their roles. The same goes for the annual performance review process. Based on Gallup's analysis of high-performing teams,[1] three qualities make performance reviews more effective:

- They focus on achievements,
- They are fair and accurate, and
- They provide developmental goals.

It's easy to say everyone is "meeting expectations." However, when someone truly goes above and beyond, it's a leader's responsibility

---

1   https://www.gallup.com/workplace/236135/
     give-performance-reviews-actually-inspire-employees.aspx

to recognize that work. When this doesn't take place, it can be very demotivating for an employee. Imagine you've spent hours and hours creating a sandcastle that could rival the Petronas Towers or the Forbidden City in awe, only to have a wave wash it all away in a matter of seconds. To see one's body of work minimalized to mediocrity or, worse, go unacknowledged is a deflating experience.

> It's easy to say everyone is "meeting expectations."
> However, when someone truly goes above and beyond,
> it's a leader's responsibility to recognize that work.

Unfortunately, this has been a part of my own career journey, and it made me feel that my contributions were not valued. One thing I've always been great at understanding is my value. Although I consider myself to be fairly long-suffering, I do have limits, and I learned that recognition of my work was something that I valued and needed from an employer. This was non-negotiable for me, and, left unaddressed, pushed me to my breaking point. It was hard to endure, and eventually I made the decision to move on.

I learned that the same was true for needing a supervisor who has your back. I realized every time I sought an external opportunity, I was ...

... FEELING UNSUPPORTED

Everyone wants to know they are supported. In a personal relationship, each individual brings their own aspirations to the table, and as they pursue their goals they want to know they have the support of their significant other. Nobody really wants to feel like they are on this journey alone. This is no different in the workplace, especially when it comes to doing your job and growing in your career.

Managers play a big part in both of these aspects of an employee's journey, and my story is no exception. I've had many managers, and some of them were better at providing support than others. When it came to career development, I had several bosses who spoke about my runway and potential, but were relaxed with the action that was necessary to take me to the next level. I strongly believe that words and actions should align. I struggled with hearing "We see you as a talent, but you should slow down and dig deeper," after which there was never any follow-through. It wasn't until I took control and made some bold decisions that I was able to see the progress I was looking for.

I don't want to give the impression that my organizations didn't invest in me. I was given the chance to lead a global expansion, work abroad, and many other amazing opportunities. I also had the good fortune to shadow some incredibly talented people. However, in many cases, I had to prompt and appeal to the "powers that be" to ensure that they followed through on those developmental opportunities. I had to own my progress, but I struggled when I tried to take these experiences to the next level and was met with the proverbial "you have a long runway," "there's still a learning curve," or "you're not ready" dialogue. This limited my organic growth and chipped away at my enthusiasm. The most frustrating part was that these statements were never coupled with guidance on how to get "ready" or minimize the "learning curve."

> I had to own my progress, but I struggled when I tried to take these experiences to the next level and was met with the proverbial "you have a long runway," "there's still a learning curve," or "you're not ready" dialogue. This limited my organic growth and chipped away at my enthusiasm.

I'd encourage everyone to take the time to reflect on these types of situations. It's easy to write off sound counsel if driven by wayward emotions. On the other hand, there is a fine line between constructive feedback and masked feedback (i.e., criticism). You have to learn the difference between the two to ensure it doesn't quench your drive and vision. In an effort to preserve my vision, I started debating on whether I needed to spread my wings and fly.

Always the optimist, I try to find the upside of situations, so I've made sure to vocalize my feelings, expectations, and the support I needed prior to leaving any organization. I want to be confident that I've made every effort possible to save the relationship, and I can say that these efforts have definitely made me take a deeper look at my abilities and knowledge. They've also helped me to better own my career and understand what I need going forward.

> **I want to be confident that I've made every effort possible to save the relationship, and I can say that these efforts have definitely made me take a deeper look at my abilities and knowledge.**

I was fortunate at one of my companies to get a glimpse of how a good leader can respond to situations like these.

Mrs. L., a.k.a. "Mama Bear," truly exhibited the characteristics of a leader. She created value, was a strong influencer, flexible, trusting, valiant through challenges, approachable ... I could go on and on. She was definitely someone you'd want to follow, who always made you feel like you had a chance to win and everything would work out in the end. I respected her so much that I adopted and leveraged several aspects of her style to better position myself in my career.

Let's face it, I'm not the most conventional HR professional; in an effort to provide the best support, I won't hesitate to ask tough questions and say things that are often left unsaid. I've always been comfortable speaking my truth, but I've learned that doing so does not always align with the traditional approach to doing business from an HR perspective. Being a leader requires a high level of maturity and ability to be open to other solutions, and I have worked with some managers who've struggled with these attributes. So, I've had to keep my style nimbler to work through these challenges to ensure I appropriately support the business' needs. More times than not, I've been able to influence and support the business with a refreshing path forward, but there have been occasions where antiquated and contemporary views on support drastically differed. Regardless of whether she agreed with my approach, Mama Bear always had my back in front of the business. She shielded me. Now, don't get me wrong, if Mama Bear felt I could handle things in a better manner, she would let me know and coach me through the situations. She didn't overlook opportunities for me to continue to improve. This empowered me to execute my role at a higher level and helped me be more organizationally savvy. Knowing I had that support made a big difference in my job satisfaction.

No one wants to be in a space where they have to question if they have the support of their leader. I have also had that experience; one manager in particular was so bad she had me doubting myself. She never took the time to get to know me and was quick to accept what other people said without properly examining things herself. My relationship with that supervisor eventually diminished to the point where our conversations only consisted of her connecting with me to provide "feedback." Furthermore, these conversations were relayed back to business leadership, which made it very difficult for me to

The E.V.O.L.V.E. Model
Step 2 – Vocalize

In Chapter 1, we explored the role of "evaluating" in the E.V.O.L.V.E. career and life ownership model. Now, let's dive into the second step — vocalize.

> *Vocalize: (verb) to give voice; to articulate; to express (a thought or emotion) in words*

Vocalization is critical in every aspect of your life, and your career is no exception. After you evaluate your career, it is important that you vocalize where you want to go in your journey, what skills you want to learn, and what thoughts you have on your next opportunity. You have to speak up. If you never say anything, how will your organization know your aspirations? Similarly, if organizations never ask or create a space for employees to share and nurture their career goals, how will they know the full potential of the talent in the organization? Without vocalization, no one will know. They can only guess.

There is power in vocalizing and following through on career aspirations. In the previous chapter, I spoke about the evaluation process, which helps you identify what you need to vocalize. However, it doesn't always help you identify the best way of communicating this information. So, let's focus on how to do just that. When you are ready to vocalize your career aspirations, consider these tips as you communicate your thoughts.

1. Prepare to communicate the information you discovered during your evaluation process and pinpoint a focus area

that is going to help you get to the next level. Identify possible development activities you would like your supervisor to support. (Note: HR is a great partner in gaining more insight on development activities for both employees and managers.)

2. Schedule a development dialogue conversation with your supervisor so you can share the information you prepared during the evaluation process. Give your supervisor enough notice so they can do their own prep work regarding how they can support you. This needs to be a two-way conversation. In addition, it is important that this meeting is designated for development topics only. Avoid connecting this discussion with project updates or performance reviews. Engage your manager. After sharing your insights and getting your manager's thoughts, make sure you align and capture a path forward on follow-up actions.

Vocalizing is also essential to improving the employee experience. You can follow a similar approach in giving feedback on your experience, compensation expectations, and other necessary topics as you do with your career aspirations. If it's a highly charged topic, I recommend gaining guidance from members of your Board of Directors or key advocates at your company. This will give you an opportunity to work through your emotions and set the tone for a productive dialogue.

partner with them and help drive the change the team so desperately needed.

This environment led me to have two overdue conversations: one with myself and one with my supervisor. I was not happy, and I was becoming more and more jaded and guarded with each passing day. I felt as if my hands were shackled and my legs were cut from under me. I had been left exposed and I took the time to articulate these feelings to my manager. Instead of things getting better, they got worse, and after I reflected on the situation and could honestly say I had done my best, I realized I had reached my breaking point. I decided it was time to pull the plug for the sake of my peace and career.

This experience made me appreciate my time with Mama Bear even more. I gained a true appreciation for the saying, "Employees don't leave their companies; they leave their managers."

Employees don't leave their companies; they leave their managers.

DEAR EMPLOYER,

Don't underestimate the power of community. Providing opportunities for your employees to create community will assist them in navigating through the good and more challenging times. Employee Resource Groups, Work Teams, and Talent Cohorts give people the chance to build relationships and find a sense of belonging in the organization. It will also provide employees with a productive space to speak up and vocalize their experiences, and find solutions to their own challenges and organizational challenges.

Have you created these types of groups for your employees? How do you promote community in your organization? How do you provide employees with a safe space to speak up? How do you ensure that people who speak up aren't negatively labeled?

....

DEAR EMPLOYEE,

Every day at work will not be perfect, but how you choose to deal with these challenging days can make a big difference in your experience. I leveraged the following techniques to get through my rough days:

- *Praying*
- *Listening to music*
- *Talking to my support group*
- *Thinking about positive things going on in my life*
- *Addressing the issues head on*

What are some of your coping resources? Do you have a work support group?

....

3

SHOULD I STAY OR SHOULD I GO

Should I stay or should I go? That's usually the headlining question when someone is considering leaving a personal relationship or an employer. However, there are many factors that you need to consider in order to fully *own* the decision you ultimately make. A relationship doesn't deteriorate on its own, and both parties have to own their part in its demise. When contemplating your decision to leave, it's important to begin with a self-evaluation. You have to determine if the situation can be fixed. Is this relationship salvageable? There are many factors that you need to consider in order to fully own the path you take. First, you need to understand the "Why." Why are you asking the question if you should stay or go? What's driving you? Is it an opportunity? Is it your peace/happiness? Is it based on the cultural fit? Whatever it is, you need to understand it so you can confidently step up or out of your organization. To answer these questions, it's important for you to be honest about your feelings before you decide whether you need to stay or go.

AM I CHASING AN OPPORTUNITY OR RUNNING FROM A PROBLEM?

One of my mentors posed this very question to me when I was debating whether to leave a company, and it made me pause. He said, "If you are running from a problem, it will follow you to your next role, company, etc., until you deal with it. If you are chasing an opportunity, then the role will present itself and timing won't be an issue." That really stuck with me and helped me demonstrate more patience and thoughtfulness when considering my next career opportunity. It also made me more confident in my decision to stay with an organization. I decided it was better to stick with the people and processes I knew versus bouncing around from company to company until I connected with the right opportunity. It gave me the time to fully assess and determine that I was not avoiding challenges in the workplace. It gave me a chance to wait until the right opportunity came along.

> If you are running from a problem, it will follow you to your next role, company, etc., until you deal with it. If you are chasing an opportunity, then the role will present itself and timing won't be an issue.

ARE YOU DISENCHANTED WITH YOUR FUNCTION, OR YOUR FUNCTION AT YOUR EMPLOYER?

In the early stages of my discontent, I considered abandoning HR to try my hand at Operations Management or Logistics. I always had an affinity for these areas as they served as my second and third majors in college. I started considering opportunities in those fields more seriously because I was dissatisfied with HR. I thought that maybe it was time to nurture my other interests more. It wasn't until I had that conversation with my friend that I realized I was asking the wrong question: "Are you disenchanted with HR, or are you disenchanted with HR *here*?"

I started processing my situation through a different lens and discovered I might have been premature in jumping the HR ship. This is a question I'd recommend to all people who are considering a new opportunity, especially one outside of your current field, whether it's HR, Finance, Sales, Operations, Marketing, or other areas. Depending on how you answer this question, there may be more internal opportunities that you could explore.

ARE YOU BEING STUNTED?

Based on my personal experience, I have seen a positive correlation between a lack of development and disengaged employees. When getting to the root cause of an employee's dissatisfaction, many express feelings of being unappreciated, unsupported, and underdeveloped. In reflecting on my own experience at a previous company, I realized that I felt stagnant in my later years at the organization. Initially my organization provided me many career-development opportunities, but none of them came with a commitment. I used to joke that my company was willing to fly me all around the world and wine and dine me, but didn't want to give me a ring. It was like I wasn't good enough.

> When getting to the root cause of an employee's dissatisfaction, many express feelings of being unappreciated, unsupported, and underdeveloped.

I started my career in a development-focused position, where I remained well beyond the expected time. Imagine being on assignment and not being sure your organization had a permanent role for you upon your return. That's a really vulnerable space to be in. I eventually landed that permanent role, but this delayed development process had a negative impact on my position at the company. Professionally, I had been pigeon-holed into my junior role. I had to work hard to rebrand and reintroduce myself to people, and it took a long time for my peers and the business to recognize me in my new position. Position authority is a real thing, and I saw and lived it. This also impacted me from a compensation standpoint, and closed doors to other opportunities within the organization based on compensation and job description guidelines. I wanted to do more, but these difficulties had a significant impact on my career growth.

HAVE YOU LEARNED WHAT YOU NEEDED TO LEARN?

Recently I connected with a friend who decided to pursue a new opportunity. I asked him what helped him make this decision and he replied, "One of my mentors told me not to look at any job as forever. Figure out what you want to learn, and once you've hit those goals decide if you want to stay or go." I like this advice and I see it as a complementary question to "Are you being stunted?" It gives you the opportunity to fully evaluate what you have learned within your role, and helps you avoid being premature in your decision to move on. It also helps to hold you accountable for your continued growth. As I mentioned earlier, you have to be in the driver seat when it comes to your career. You should have a general understanding, at a minimum, of what you want to get out of each role you take.

Don't look at any job as forever. Figure out what
you want to learn, and once you've hit those
goals decide if you want to stay or go.

DEAR EMPLOYER,

Should I stay or should I go? That's not your question to answer, in this case, but you can influence how your employees respond. First you must understand the "Why." Why will you appeal as the employer of choice? What's going to make people want to stay? Here are five questions you can answer to support your quest to retain talent:

1. *Do you understand the needs of your employees? Don't let your talent get to a point where they are questioning, "Should I stay or should I go?"*

2. *Are you regularly keeping a pulse on your employee engagement? Are you leveraging "stay interviews" to better understand why employees stay or want to leave? Do you recognize the value of your talent and actively tell them how they impact the organization?*

3. *How would you define your company culture? Is it a place where talent can thrive? Is your culture welcoming, or does it support an environment of isolation? Continue to evaluate your company culture.*

4. *Are you empowering your leaders to lead and your employees to own their careers? Are you holding bad leaders accountable?*

5. *Do you take measurable, timely action once you've identified retention issues?*

Ask yourself the tough questions and do the required work to create an environment where people want to stay. You have to keep dating! All the things you did and highlighted about your company to help attract talent will help you retain them if you keep the same level of engagement.

The E.V.O.L.V.E. Model
Step 3 – Own

We've explored how to evaluate and vocalize in our careers. Now, let's talk about how to own your decisions.

> *Own: (verb) to admit or acknowledge that something is the case or that one feels a certain way*

Ownership is where a decision meets accountability. Whatever decision you make, you have to own it. You have a say in how each situation turns out — whether you are an employee, or you are the employer. As a leader, if you see opportunities to engage talent but prioritize other needs before it, that's fine. However, you have to own what that could mean for your organization.

There is very little in life that just happens to us. It's more about how we respond to the things that are happening, and how we control the things we have the power to control. At the end of the day, whether the results are positive or negative, each decision you make is on you and you have to be okay with that.

ARE YOU HAPPY?

Before I joined Corporate America, I made a promise to myself that if my work stopped being fun and I found myself complaining more than enjoying the experience, then I would look to move on. Clearly, I found myself in that space or I wouldn't be writing this

In regard to career ownership, there are many ways you can own your experience. One way is to start with establishing a vision for your career.

What do you want to be when you grow up?

That's one of the hardest questions I know because you have to marry your aspirations, abilities, work ethic and perseverance to make it happen. However, it becomes a lot easier to grow when you know what direction you are going in, and how each decision will allow you to experience more freedom in your career and life journey.

Where are you on your career ownership journey? Are you reflecting or deflecting?

Think about these questions. And get honest about what opportunities await, if you'll only "own" your decisions, behaviors, words, and attitudes.

book. Instead of staying and having a potentially negative impact on my team or my career, I made the decisions to leave. Even with this understanding, they were still hard decisions to make because I'd had so many happy times at most of my previous companies. But I knew that a lot of those happy moments were connected to the relationships I had built with my teammates and the business, and not because of the companies themselves.

> I made a promise to myself that if my work stopped being fun and I found myself complaining more than enjoying the experience, then I would look to move on.

Teammate or relationship departure guilt is a real thing. Though deciding to leave or stay was my decision alone, I definitely took into account who I would be leaving behind. Some of the things I asked myself were: "Am I leaving the team hanging?" "Who's going to take care of my Business Units like me?" "What will my boss think about my decision?" "Will I ever find awesome teammates like this again?" "Who will be my shade buddies?"

My former colleagues had become more than just colleagues over the years. We had developed friendships that went beyond the end of our work days. We had a genuine respect, appreciation, and love for one another. They supported me through so many life changes and were a part of my career journey, cheering me on or sitting me down to tell me "how the cow eats cabbage." They provided me with a comfortable space that I was reluctant to leave. They helped me endure.

Then there were my business partners, a few of whom I truly enjoyed supporting as they challenged me to think bigger, be better, and operate in a space of collaboration. My business leaders' styles were admirable and inspirational and, in many ways, they helped me elevate my own level of support. When you have partnerships like that, it's hard to walk away, but I knew I had reached a plateau that would eventually hinder my career growth. Although I knew what I needed to do, it still didn't make leaving these relationships any easier.

Then there was my supervisor. As I shared earlier, Mama Bear was a true leader. She went to bat for all of her people, yet also was sure to hold us accountable. She covered us and didn't leave us exposed to some of the misguided darts of the business. Deep down I knew she would be disappointed about my decision to leave, but would still be supportive of my needs and goals, and I was right. I will never forget her walking me to my car on my last day, giving me a hug, and telling me to "Go kick ass!" She promised to keep in touch and she has. Quite frankly, I really wish I'd had more time under her tutelage, but she came too late in the fourth quarter of my career love game. Even her support and efforts couldn't push this into overtime. The time had expired and the decision was made; it was time to "break up."

....

DEAR EMPLOYER,

To counter or to not counter … that is the question.

Counter offers are usually reserved for top talent and high performers, but they can be a roll of the dice. From an employee's perspective, as you'll read in the upcoming testimonials, some people appreciate the effort that an organization goes through to retain them, while others question why the effort wasn't made earlier.

You won't be able to save every talent, but the probability of doing so is much higher if you are proactive in your efforts. Take the time to focus on having solid development plans, ensuring compensation equity, driving employee engagement, and, most importantly, following through on commitments you've made to your employees. As an organization, you play a major part in the employee experience. If you haven't exhausted every effort to create an environment conducive to success for all, then you have to own what that may mean for your organization ... positive or negative results, like staffing instability, culture voyeurism, vacillating profits, etc.

What proactive measures are you taking to ensure you retain your talent? Do you have a company position on counter-offers?

. . . .

DEAR EMPLOYEE,

Should I Stay or Should I Go Self-Assessment

Use this form to evaluate and record your thoughts. Candidly reflect on these questions to determine whether you should stay or go.

Are you chasing an opportunity or running from a problem?
Are you disenchanted with your function or your function at your employer?

Are you being stunted?

Are there still things you need to learn?

LIAM'S TESTIMONIAL:
Let's Stay Together

I'm sooo in love with you ... perhaps that's a bit heavy for the moment, but love was definitely in the air when my friend, Liam, started as a Recruiting Assistant on February 14, 2011. Although it was an entry-level position, Liam was excited for the chance to leave his current company, which he felt had questionable working practices. He was excited for the flexibility and seemingly limitless opportunities that lay ahead. Liam made an immediate impact in his role by leveraging his previous years of recruiting experience and channeling that into ways to anticipate and proactively respond to the needs of the three recruiters he was supporting. When a recruiting role became available within a month of Liam joining the company, he applied and got the job.

Over the next three and a half years, Liam worked his way up to a mid-level recruiting role through his continuous demonstration of high performance, which was recognized by high performance ratings. In fact, Liam received the unicorn of performance rating scores when he earned the highest rating you could receive, an "Outstanding-1". Although his work was being recognized through the performance system, Liam still yearned for deeper development dialogue discussions and more exposure to upper management.

"I felt I was seen favorably, but that was never really verbalized. I had aspirations to continue my career growth, but wasn't thinking about leaving the organization. Then one day a former colleague reached out to me about a great Senior Recruiter opportunity at his organization. The new role would provide a $20,000 bump in pay, higher bonuses, and more responsibilities. Within four weeks, I had an offer in my hand. After weighing my options and seeing the experience I'd be able to gain, I decided to accept the other company's offer.

I informed my current employer of my decision, and was met with shock. It was the first time I was finally hearing how the organization viewed me. I learned that I had been identified as a "High-Potential" employee, and the Head of Talent Acquisition shared the succession plans they had identified for me on the Recruiting and HR Business Partner path, which I wanted to explore. She also shared with me a development roadmap and told me that if I stayed, they would help me get to the next level, and that my compensation would reflect that.

I left that meeting with a commitment from the Head of Talent Acquisition that she would follow up with a counteroffer. The next day, which was unheard of given stringent approval processes, I had an offer in hand that included a two-grade/band-level jump, a $20,000 pay increase, a one-year retention bonus, and a commitment for me to be able to participate in the company's Leadership Academy abroad in order to gain even more exposure. I was also made privy to the approval email chain showing the commitment to me from other levels of the organization. I was beyond moved by the efforts taken on my behalf. My commitment to the company grew ten-fold, and I knew that was where I wanted to be."

Liam reached out to the other company to let them know that his current company had made a counteroffer, and he was planning on staying. Interestingly enough, the other company countered with another offer, but after he declined again, he got a sign that showed him he made the right decision. Their Head of Recruitment asked him, "Do you know the statistics behind employees who accept a counteroffer from their company? They will set expectations you can't meet and you will end up leaving the company in a year." Liam didn't like how she tried to use this to shame him for his decision. It was in that moment that he knew he had made the right decision.

Liam's company proceeded to follow through on their commitment. He was pulled into the Recruiting Transformation implementation as a subject-matter expert. Within a year he was promoted to a Senior Recruiter II and gained more exposure with the HR Leadership Team. By late 2015, Liam was preparing to start a short-term assignment as an HR Business Partner.

He shared, "I was given a mentor to support me in my short-term assignment, which was nice. My new boss also shared that I had come highly recommended by HR leadership and that they were committed to developing me over the next four months."

Liam saw great success in his interim role and when a permanent HR Business Partner role become available, he applied. He took a one-grade-level demotion to move into this position, but within seven months he had been promoted back to his previous level.

"I continued to grow as an HR Business Partner, transitioning from being operational to more strategic. I was able to become a trusted partner to the business, and my work continued to receive recognition in the HR space. So much so that my name came up in a Talent Review to lead an integration. In this role, I would be a direct report of an HR leadership team member, gain Merger & Acquisition experience, and gain executive-level client experience with support responsibility for four Executive Leaders. When I look back on how my career has flourished in the past four years, I am glad I decided to stay."

Based on his experience, Liam shared the following advice:

1. Before you seek a new opportunity outside of your organization, have an open/candid conversation about potential growth opportunities within your current company.

2. Develop a strong relationship with your manager. If you are not comfortable doing that, you have to consider if you are in the right place.

3. Work to obtain development/promotional opportunities without giving ultimatums. Get a pulse on your manager's support and be realistic about how you are perceived. It's important to have "Commitment Reciprocity."

4. See if you've still got it. It's okay to test the market and see what's out there in order to gauge how you are received.

5. Push yourself to move outside of your comfort zone.

4

LET'S BREAK UP

So you've finally come to the conclusion that this situation is not going to work for you anymore. Let's focus on how you are going to leave. Break-ups can range from simple to complicated, based on the circumstances of the situation. Regardless of which end of the spectrum you find yourself on, there are both wrong and right ways to end things, and it's important to get it right.

NOTICE PERIOD

It is customary to give two weeks' notice before departing an organization. Unless the situation is dire, or if more harm will be done by staying any longer, you want to try to adhere to the two-week rule. Depending on the relationship, you might even want to give a longer notice period, if possible. I have been on both sides of this situation, as the person leaving and as the person needing to fill the role, so I know the difference adequate notice can make, especially if the individual is working on key initiatives that will take a longer time to transition to others. Keep in mind, however, that this decision should not be made to the detriment of your new opportunity. When you are transitioning to a new opportunity, your allegiance should shift to what lies before you.

> **When you are transitioning to a new opportunity, your allegiance should shift to what lies before you.**

Now let's discuss if the split is not amicable. I used to be a firm believer in the "it doesn't matter, give them two weeks" philosophy, until I found myself in a very toxic situation. I was facing moving performance targets and my business managers were deflecting their leadership and performance inadequacies on me. I was in a culture that excused bad behavior as long as we were "winning," and had a poor HR support system. The environment did not align with my values and expectations for an employer. I debated on giving a one-week notice, or even no notice at all — it was that bad. However, some of my close confidants persuaded me to not take that approach. I yielded to their counsel and provided a two-week notice. Fortunately, I was on vacation during most of that time, so it was a win/win.

When I told my manager I was leaving, it felt like physical weights were being lifted off of me. I felt a sense of serenity and happiness. I felt ***liberated***. At the end of the day, you have to do what's best for you and be able to live with the decision you make. It's a small world and how you handle a departure could come back to impact you later on, but you have to do what's best for your peace and sanity.

> **At the end of the day, you have to do what's best for you and be able to live with the decision you make.**

FACE-TO-FACE VS. EAR-TO-EAR VS. EMAIL

Abandoning your job or sending an email to say you are quitting is kind of like disappearing on your partner or breaking up with them over a text message. It is seen as one of the weakest moves you can make, and it's sure to leave the other party extremely annoyed or, worse, infuriated. I've never been in a situation where I've considered this approach. Even when I debated on giving no notice, I was still going to have a conversation. When I left my companies, I told my supervisors face-to-face or via telephone, and followed up with a resignation letter. Ideally, I prefer to have these conversations in person, but certain circumstances can necessitate communicating your resignation over telephone. In one instance, my manager was out of the country and I wanted to give her as much time as possible to start looking for my replacement and to support knowledge transfer. On another occasion, my supervisor and I were based at different locations.

I started telling my peers and business leaders only after notifying my supervisors. As I mentioned earlier, I had built strong relationships with these people, so it was important for me to share this news on my own and in my own way.

KNOWLEDGE TRANSFER

Knowledge transfer is one of the best gifts you can leave behind when leaving an organization. More than likely you will not be able to wrap up all of your responsibilities before you leave, but you can assist in a smooth transition. I put together a document that outlined the key objectives of my position and where I was in the process of achieving them. I held a meeting with my peers and supervisor to go over the objectives and address any questions they had, and afterward left them to cast lots for my workload.

> **Knowledge transfer is one of the best gifts you can leave behind when leaving an organization.**

YOU ARE REPRESENTING YOURSELF

Some people asked me why I went the extra mile when I knew I was moving on. To that I replied, "Because it still has my name attached to it." I'm a firm believer in running through the finish line. At the end of the day, your work represents your brand and your brand represents your name. When it's all said and done, you don't want to undermine your contributions or your brand. It's very important to keep your feelings about the situation and the long-term impact of your work separate. There were some things I was not pleased with upon my departure, but I did not let it affect my work during my exit. To me, it speaks to your professionalism and maturity. I'm not saying to overwork yourself in the final days, but use your judgment; you will know what is appropriate during that time.

> **At the end of the day, your work represents your brand and your brand represents your name. When it's all said and done, you don't want to undermine your contributions or your brand.**

BRIDGES GO TWO WAYS FOR A REASON

Another reason I am mindful of my exits is because you never know when you'll have to cross that bridge again. Bridges go two ways for a reason. You may never want to return to a previous employer, but you never know when circumstances might arise that would make doing so a good career move. It is important not to ruin relationships on your way out the door. We also know we live in a small world. You never know who knows whom and you don't want to leave a negative impression. This can be hard. Trust me, I've had moments where I wanted to burn the bridge, kick the board game, and go out with a bang. But after I had my moment and talked it through with a few people, I came back to myself. You may get a lot of satisfaction out of adding fireworks to your exit, but nine times out of ten, you'll regret it. (But cheers to the one time it does work ... you're the real MVP!)

> **It is important not to ruin relationships on your way out the door.**

SECURE A NEW OPPORTUNITY FIRST

When it's time to leave, make sure you have a new opportunity in place. It doesn't necessarily have to be with another company — you can start your own thing. But you should have concrete plans about what you want to do next, unless you are economically independent ... in which case you'll have a little more flexibility.

Have you noticed that when you are single, it seems like no one wants you, but as soon as you announce you're dating someone, you learn about all these people who wanted to be with you? That's how it works in Corporate America, too. It is easier to find another opportunity when you have a job; it makes you more attractive to the next organization. I looked for opportunities while I continued to fulfill the duties of my current role. I only made the leap after I connected with the right opportunity. I made the decision to continue in an environment I knew instead of quickly jumping to an interim role, embracing my mentor's words about chasing an opportunity instead

The E.V.O.L.V.E. Model
Step 4 – Liberate

It's time to touch on how following the E.V.O.L.V.E. process can bring about a different level of freedom ... how it can leave you liberated!

> *Liberate: (verb) release from a state or situation that limits freedom of thought or behavior*

Whether you leave or stay in a position, you should have a sense of freedom in your ability to be your best self. Moving without fear is a part of my spiritual DNA, and I have seen and felt the benefits of operating my career that way. That's why it's important that you prevent anything from hindering your ability to feel free to thrive. From a career ownership standpoint, no job should consistently make you feel like you are serving a life sentence. Yes, there will be tough days, but no job should rob you of your peace, happiness, or ability to fulfill your purpose.

of "running from a problem." It also gave me time to process through some lingering feelings before transitioning to my new role.

DEAR EMPLOYER,

More often than not, when a couple breaks up there are things that both parties have to own regarding the demise of the relationship.

There is power in being liberated. When you are able to deal with the things that are holding you back, you start to see opportunities in places once unknown to you. As you continue to evaluate, vocalize, and own your decisions, you position yourself to better claim and maintain your professional liberation.

One of the reasons I wrote this book was to share the possibility of liberation with you. I know what it's like to be in a toxic working environment and I'm proud to have made the decision to free myself from that situation. I had to first make the decision to give myself permission to leave, and it wasn't as easy as you'd expect. The E.V.O.L.V.E. model works; if you evaluate, vocalize, and own your career, you will be able to liberate yourself from toxic situations, should they arise.

Similarly, there are things that corporations can do better when it comes to retaining their talent and gaining useful insight from employee departures. Exit interviews are often used to get a better understanding of why people are leaving, but they are reactive mechanisms that may only give you limited feedback, if any at all. Often, departing employees will filter their feedback so you can't get to the heart of the reason they are leaving. Alternatively, some people are extremely brutal in their comments to the point that it raises questions about the validity of the feedback. Because of this, I recommend that a Talent Loss Review is coupled with the exit interview. A Talent Loss Review is a comprehensive assessment of departing talent (e.g., the employee's development plan, performance, grade/band level, years of service, etc.) that is done to help you identify any trends among exiting employees. Coupled with your exit interview and proactive employee engagement/retention efforts, the Talent Loss Review will assist in making more informed decisions about your talent retention strategy. Your key takeaway is action ... you have to follow up and make necessary changes, or none of these efforts will matter.

....

DEAR EMPLOYEE,

More often than not, when a couple breaks up there are things that both parties have to own regarding the demise of the relationship. Similarly, the same thing can apply to a work relationship. As an HR professional I have seen and supported employees who've made decisions to leave their companies based on struggles that could impact their experience at any *employer, if they go unaddressed:*

1. ***Entitlement Mentality*** *– Some employees have an insatiable list of expectations they want their employer to meet. Nothing is ever enough, and it often contributes to hindering the employee's experiences at a company. I'm not saying you shouldn't have standards, but it's important to be realistic about your expectations.*

2. ***The Comparison Trap*** *– Focusing on your talent, growth, and success relative to your colleagues' is a dangerous habit. You can never fully know all the details of that person's journey, or sacrifices they've had to make to get where they are. I recommend focusing on* your own *growth and what* you *bring to the table. I've*

also found that when I've stopped to give thanks and reflect on all that I've accomplished, it's helped me refocus on my journey.

3. ***Closed-Mouth Syndrome*** *– There is a saying that "closed mouths don't get fed," and it's true. If you are looking for a new opportunity or are having challenges in the workplace but never tell anyone, how is your company supposed to know? How can they take action? The same goes for exploring your interests and showcasing your work. If you keep these things to yourself, or let others take the credit for your work, then no one will ever know. You have to advocate for yourself.*

If you fall into any of these categories, take a step back and re-evaluate whether it's time to move on.

• •

GLORY'S TESTIMONIAL:
A Survivor

Now that you're out of my life, I'm so much better ... but it didn't start that way for my friend Glory. Glory has been specializing in the HR Benefits and Compensation space for about five years and currently works as an HR Manager at a small change consultant firm. This path had not been her original career plan, but in retrospect was the perfect path for her all along.

Glory graduated with an undergraduate degree in International Business and had dreams to travel and conduct business on behalf of global companies. She didn't know how to make her dreams a reality, and she didn't have real guidance on how to navigate these goals. She had no internships. No connections. No network. But she did have family. Her grandfather, affectionately known as Poppy, was very instrumental in helping her start her career. He introduced her to a network of individuals who saw the potential within her, and supported her decision to return to school for her MBA, with a concentration in HR, only a year after receiving her undergraduate degree.

When Glory enrolled in graduate school, she was also continuing to settle into her new role as a mother of a three-month-old. It was a very exciting time in her life and it was around this time that she recalls finding her dream company.

Glory shared, "I happened to be at a gathering on a small boat with my grandfather and I saw this beautiful building right on the shore. I told him that I was going to work there. I had no idea what company it was or what they did, I just saw glitz and glamour and I wanted to be a part of it. Two months later, I was hired as a contractor at that company in a college-recruiting position. This move officially set the trajectory for my new career path. I stayed in that role for a year and a half, and it ended up expanding far beyond what anyone thought it would be."

This role opened the door for Glory's HR career, and she had no intention of turning back. This was her dream organization. A year and a half after she started, she was offered an opportunity in a "fast track program." This required her to relocate from the company's headquarters, but the outcome would be to receive an HR Leader position within a three-year timeframe. She accepted the offer and moved. In hindsight, she describes it as "the worst decision of her life."

She had early indicators that things weren't going to work out. There was a lot confusion around her initial site visit due to poor communications and because she never received an itinerary. Her visit lasted all of two hours and she went home with a sense of reluctance about taking the role. However, after speaking with another African-American employee who was based at the new location, she was sold on taking the opportunity. She moved, but little did she know that this person was going to leave the organization and take with them a key piece of her support system at that location. She tried to assimilate into her new role and community, but quickly realized she was in an extremely racially-suppressed environment. The deal-breaker was when a "flag rally" was held outside her gated community, where Confederate flags were being proudly waved by the demonstrators. Glory couldn't leave and felt unsafe. She expressed her concerns to the development program organizer and was told that if she left that location, she would no longer be employed by the company. Interestingly enough, there was a similar situation at the company involving a Caucasian employee who was placed in a city predominately populated by African Americans and that was often portrayed as dangerous. Prior to being assigned to this location, that employee was provided provisions in case she ever felt unsafe, without request.

Glory began the pursuit to keep her job as she fought to get out of this unsafe environment and back to the company's headquarters.

She shared, "It was not easy. I thought about leaving then. I questioned if I should stay with the company based on the fact that a committee of people had chosen a location for me to begin this program without considering the racial difficulties I might encounter."

Ultimately, reason prevailed. Influential leaders in the organization intervened and Glory returned to a specialized role in Compensation and Benefits at the company's headquarters. This role had not been a part of her career plan, but it got her out of the unsafe environment and secured her continued employment with the company. Unfortunately, the situation still had a negative impact on Glory's happiness at the company.

"I came to this role and was bitter. I had inadequate training, an uninviting team, and it was very different from what I was used to. I was excluded in many ways, and I never felt comfortable sharing this with others. I was now in a position where I was heavily supervised, from the time I arrived at work to the timeliness of my email responses, along with many other things that were now being asked of me. I was in a very dark space for close to two years. It made me upset that I was on the first page of the company's website, I was doing great work within and outside of my team, but I was not able to fully be myself. Then I began to see differences in how I was treated as compared to some of my teammates, one of whom was the same age as me but lacked the education and experience (no MBA and limited HR exposure). I saw that he was fully included and embraced as a team *member*, versus my treatment as simply a team *worker*. I knew then that I had to leave; the question was how and where would I go?"

At this time, Glory pulled from previous conversations she'd had with her grandfather about creating strong connections, and she started looking for other opportunities.

"At the point I decided to leave, I had connected with everyone in the business. According to my leaders, I was not performing well, but I had made every course correction I could possibly think of. I had exhausted every option, every suggestion that came to me.

It came to a point where I was crying in my car before I walked into my office. I was under an overwhelming amount of pressure created by my leaders and by broken processes that paralyzed me from doing my job. This was also coupled with a performance review that was the most outrageous and unprofessional review I had ever received. I was threatened with a performance plan, and at the end of the meeting I was also told that I would be picking up additional responsibilities because another employee had resigned from the company. I walked out of that meeting broken. Absolutely broken! I was told I was not good enough to be paid more for my work after three years and that I was not performing well, BUT I was good enough to take on the responsibilities of someone else's job. I had a harsh realization that this was not about performance, education, work ethic, or any of that; I realized that this company had no idea what to do with a young, intelligent black woman. This company would not allow me to go further in my career, and I decided I was not going to allow this negative environment to diminish my worth."

Eight weeks later, Glory started in a new role with a smaller company. Interestingly enough, efforts were made to retain her at her previous employer when a Senior Leader intervened on her behalf.

"I really appreciated his efforts. It was another sign that someone saw my value and I was doing the right things. But I couldn't stay after everything that had happened, and I didn't want to be given another role simply because a Senior Leader had to intervene. I left with some closure from that perspective. I moved to an organization that recognized my value and saw me as the HR professional I always knew I was."

Based on her experience, Glory shared the following advice:

- For Employees:

  - **Advocate for yourself.** That's one of the things I should have done that I didn't do.

  - **Know when it's time to leave.** I regret not leaving sooner. The toxic interactions and day-to-day turmoil had become so common that it turned into a pattern. I became used to it. Leaving was my best decision.

- For Employers:

  - **Don't turn a blind eye to bad managers.** There are inadequate managers, and there are also managers with unconscious and conscious biases toward African-American talent and that of other people of color. If we want to talk and implement diversity and inclusion, we have to consciously create an environment to help that talent succeed. It is imperative that any employer, big or small, recognize when a manager has a bad track record with diverse talent. Employers have to be willing to be vulnerable and admit that some managers rarely interact with diverse people, especially people of color, and that can impact how they lead this talent. Success plans for both parties can be overkill, but they can also be seen as plans of action. Are you willing to take the risk for what the manager brings to the company versus retaining a talent that could be the future of your organization? What risk is the company willing to take?

— **Don't get in your own way.** Don't ignore the signs that you need to do something.

5

LIFE AFTER THE BREAK-UP

Before moving on from any personal relationship you need to deal with unresolved feelings, and switching companies is no different. While I was going through my transition periods, I always took some time to reflect on my experiences. I learned how to be a true Business Partner, a Collaborator, and a Broker. My ability to execute on HR support and initiatives far exceeded the compensation and growth opportunities presented to me. During my experience, this was a bitter pill to swallow, but once removed I was able to find a bright side to these situations. I was walking away with a lot of knowledge that would support me in being a better HR professional and that would help me set appropriate expectations before joining a new company.

RESPECTING TIME

I learned to respect time. With my former employers, their time was their time and my time became their time, too. This was not their fault, but I was conditioned early on by the unspoken rule of always staying connected. There were many early mornings and late nights,

and all for what? In my reflection, I asked myself if this time invest-
ment was really necessary and did it add value? In some cases, the
answer was yes. When a job needed to get done, I was going to find
a way to get it done. In other cases, the answer was no, as I started
to become more efficient. However, I found that increases in performance usually gave my supervisors the signal to give me more and
more work under the guise of "development."

First let me clarify, more work does not always equate to development. There is a misconception that if you give an employee more
work, that it's surely developing them. I'd argue that unless that additional work is aligned with the individual's development goals, then
it can actually hinder growth because it takes the employee's focus
away from their goals. Because of this, I am more mindful and selec-
tive of projects I take on, and I am more likely to have a conversation
about my workload when it has exceeded a certain threshold. This
has allowed me to be more efficient and better execute on my core
projects and initiatives. I have my former employers to thank for that.

> **Unless additional work is aligned with an
> individual's development goals, then it can
> actually hinder growth because it takes the
> employee's focus away from their goals.**

When it comes to time, I have also learned to respect my personal
time in the evenings and on vacation. I admit, I still check my email
when I'm "off" work, but I have reduced the number of times I do
that. One of the reasons I continue this practice is to provide support
during off shifts and for other regions, but I try to manage the
frequency of my connection to my phone.

As for vacation, I was proud when I took my first vacation where
I didn't answer one email or phone call. It wasn't easy, but I've

learned it's important to take that time to refresh
the situation from the perspective of knowing that I regu
an honest, full day of work and I respect that time, so I need to ს.
respecting my own time, or no one else will. It was quite invigorating
to remain disconnected during my vacation and guess what? There
were no fires and everything was fine when I returned. Go figure. At
the end of the day, self-care is not an option — it's mandatory. If you
are empty, you can't pour into anyone else.

> **At the end of the day, self-care is not an
> option — it's mandatory. If you are empty,
> you can't pour into anyone else.**

GETTING RID OF THE BAGGAGE

As I mentioned earlier, you have to deal with unresolved feelings
about your employment or you will take them with you to your
next company. I was upset about how some things transpired at
my previous companies. There were certain situations that I felt
weren't handled properly. Great work went unnoticed or was down-
played. The total failure of one of my bosses as a leader didn't sit
well with me either. I had feelings of frustration, confusion, anger,
and sadness, all of which I had to deal with before I moved on.
I had to reconcile why things transpired the way they did … right,
wrong, or indifferent. Prior to leaving I had an opportunity to
purge negative energy and make room for positive thoughts. At
one company, I literally went through my room and found every
company-emblazoned product and threw it in a box. On my last day,
I left that box in my office and didn't look back. It gave me closure
and helped me put forth my best self for the next company.

ORGANIZATIONAL REVIEW: NON-NEGOTIABLES

- Good Benefits
- Talent Development
- Fair Practices
- Consistent
- Value Diversity & Inclusion
- Leadership
- Work-Life Balance
- Respect
- Autonomy
- Sustainable
- Safety Focus

- Manager/Employee Relationship
- Results Driven
- Customer Focus
- Employee Focus
- Accountability
- Integrity
- Community Commitment
- Risk-Free
- Brand Recognition
- Flexibility
- Wellbeing/Health

- Equal Opportunity
- Growth
- Recognition
- Compensation Equity
- Transparency
- Innovative
- Fun
- Inclusive Business Culture
- Anti-Hierarchical
- Meritocracy
- Employee Education Assistance

List eight characteristics you expect your organization to demonstrate:

1.   5.

2.   6.

3.   7.

4.   8.

Reflect on why you selected the above characteristics:

Describe how your current or potential employer aligns with these characteristics:

FORGIVING AND CELEBRATING

In personal relationships, they say if you can pass the following tests, then you have really moved on after a break-up. I see no difference in moving on from a former employer. These tests are applicable litmus tests for gauging your ability to move on:

1. The First-Emotion Test

Do positive or negative emotions come up when you think about your past job? Does it still sting? I can confidently say I've passed this test. When I think about my previous employers, I think about the people and some of the amazing opportunities the companies provided me. One opportunity in particular gave me the foundation I needed to execute on some of my current initiatives with my new employer. In addition, these opportunities enabled me to connect with people from other cultures in a more professional and personal way. I'm truly thankful for these experiences.

2. The Connection Test

Are you able to stay connected in a positive manner? When it comes to the connection test, I still associate with people from my previous organizations. I've built some strong relationships and if they need help from me, or vice versa, that support is still there. I left my previous organizations with blessings from so many people and I left peace with them. Just because I switched companies doesn't mean our friendships expired. I honored those connections when I was there and that continues now that I'm gone.

3. The "I Wish You Well" Test

Do you want to see your former employer or its people fail? One of my previous employers is having record-breaking success and I love to see them win. I believed in their products while I was there and still do now that I'm gone. It brings me joy to know that I was a part of building that success over the years, and that they continue to do great things. Furthermore, I'm just not wired to sit and hope for another person's failure, and I pray I never get to that space. That type of negative energy usually ends up consuming you and will prevent you from the embracing the blessings awaiting you. It's ok to applaud someone else's success, even if they don't clap for you.

4. Your Overall Thoughts Test

Overall, was it good or bad? I can honestly smile when I think about many of my experiences with former employers. I thank them for giving me an opportunity to grow and learn what type of HR Business Partner I want to be. I thank them for helping me identify what type of leader I do and do not want to be. I thank them for helping me meet some wonderful people ... my HR-ettes, an extended HR cast, and some dynamic, progressive leaders.

My ability to process my feelings and effectively move on also ***validated*** my decisions to leave in many ways. I believe I was able to pass

The E.V.O.L.V.E. Model
Step 5 – Validate

As you have seen, the "stay or go" decision at work is a universally relatable but highly personal experience. I believe the E.V.O.L.V.E. model of career and life owner-ship helps put action and structure to a disorienting time. I hope you have begun to learn and will continue to learn skills you can use in your career journey. Let's explore step 5 of the E.V.O.L.V.E. model: validate.

Validate: (verb) to demonstrate or support the truth or value of something

Validation is the confirmation that signifies that you have made the right decision. It endorses the effectiveness of your evaluation, vocalization, and ownership process. Liberation is a direct verification you made the right call. In my career journey, I often recognize my ability to move on — taking the good and processing the bad — as an indication I made the right decision. The four-part litmus test in this chapter should help you assess your ability to move on.

Each of the questions asked in the test are important to help you determine if you can validate your decision, and if you are ready to elevate to the next level.

these tests because I left before it was too late. There is a point of no return, and you want to make sure you don't go beyond that posi-tion. My ability to honestly evaluate my level of disengagement, and my organization's inability to act on certain situations, helped me save these relationships. Had I not made the decisions to move on, I guarantee you bridges would have been burned and roads would've been destroyed. What's the value in that? Avoiding this path speaks to your level of maturity and ability to set aside your wounded feelings, see the other side, and come to the conclusion that separation is necessary. That type of maturity, at most, makes it possible for all parties to remain amicable during and after the break-up, and at the very least, helps you move on. It also opens you up for your next opportunity.

HAVE YOU MOVED ON?

Take some time to reflect on your previous organization. Write down your immediate thoughts.

The First-Emotion Test – Are your first emotions positive or negative? Why?

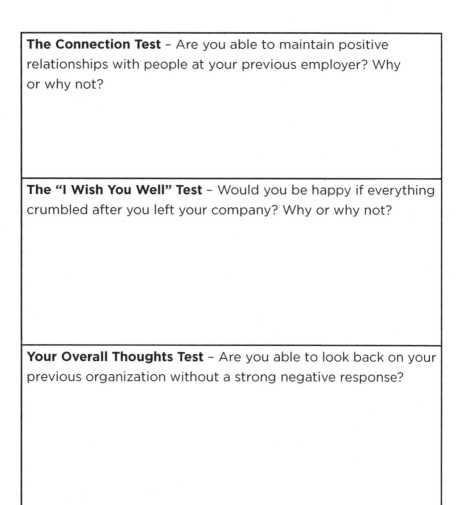

The Connection Test – Are you able to maintain positive relationships with people at your previous employer? Why or why not?

The "I Wish You Well" Test – Would you be happy if everything crumbled after you left your company? Why or why not?

Your Overall Thoughts Test – Are you able to look back on your previous organization without a strong negative response?

If you answered yes to most of these questions, then you can confidently say you have moved on. If not, that's fine too. Just continue to reflect and process your experience so you can move forward. It's important to process your feelings before you move to your next opportunity.

6

I'M DATING AGAIN

Unless you decide otherwise, most people waste no time transitioning to their new opportunity. I was no different. Two weeks after breaking up with my previous employer, I was putting my HR superpowers to good use somewhere else. I'd be lying if I said it wasn't an adjustment. I learned many things when transitioning to my new role like:

GIVE YOURSELF TIME

This is a big change. For the most part, everything is new … a new company, new colleagues, often a new location, and new ambiguity. It will take some time to operate at your regular level. In my case the learning curve decreased exponentially. I moved into a newly created role so I was able to establish a strong partnership immediately with my support . During this time, I met with key stakeholders, learned key processes, and had a chance to settle into my position. I know this approach isn't always possible, but it helps to be able to pace yourself. Give yourself the time to familiarize yourself with everything. In most cases you will be operating at normal in no time.

DON'T MAKE A COPY OF THE ORIGINAL

Your new employer is not a redo of your old company. Don't try to duplicate everything you experienced at your former employer. Instead leverage those experiences to leave a new footprint. When

The E.V.O.L.V.E. Model
Step 6 – Elevate

As you progress through the steps of the E.V.O.L.V.E. model, you're likely to feel like you are moving forward and upward — like you're taking a career elevator to the top. Step 6 is all about that elevation.

> *Elevate: (verb) raise to a more important or impressive level*

Elevation is required as you continue to progress and evolve in your career. The current version of you will not be able to appropriately support the next level you are trying to ascend to if you aren't finding ways to elevate. It's important to continuously look for ways to get better — in your skillset, in your leadership, in your knowledge, in your attitudes, and, overall, in your career.

As you continue to E.V.O.L.V.E., your growth will be built on the foundation of your ability to evaluate, vocalize, own, liberate, and validate the decisions you make. And each decision has the power to elevate you. Utilizing this process will put you in the best position to completely own your life and career.

I started with my new employers, the first thing I did was listen and learn. It was important for me to learn the people, processes, policies, and procedures (the "4Ps"). This helped me get a better understanding of my new employers, and of improvements I could put in place to enhance the 4Ps.

> **Don't try to duplicate everything you experienced at your former employer. Instead leverage those experiences to leave a new footprint.**

BUILD RELATIONSHIPS AND LEARN YOUR ROLE

I've spoke briefly about the 4Ps, but I want to spend a little more time on one P in particular: People. Building relationships is important no matter what role you take. I'd argue that the better you are at building relationships, the better your career will be. Your engagement with your peers, direct reports, manager, leadership, and other key stakeholders is critical, so take the time to understand and nurture those relationships. This is important throughout your whole career, but it is especially critical as you lay the appropriate foundation for a new role. One way to do this is to learn about your position so that you have a better understanding of the best way to articulate your ideas, contributions, and ultimately your value. Beyond the importance of knowledge transfer, I'd also suggest connecting with people who can share "tribal" knowledge. These people are great resources for learning the good, bad, and ugly about your new organization, but be sure to use their feedback simply as a reference point. It's still important that you form your own opinion about your company.

> Your engagement with your peers, direct
> reports, manager, leadership, and other key
> stakeholders is critical, so take the time to
> understand and nurture those relationships.

CAREER ROADMAP – PERSONAL OPERATING MODEL

As I shared earlier, it's important to have a vision about where you want to take your career, and that you continually work to bring that vision to fruition. Understanding how your new role fits into your career roadmap is essential. Be sure to take time to reflect on what you want to get out of this opportunity, such as enhanced leadership capabilities, new relationships, competency development, etc. Every role is critical to ensuring you get the most out of your career journey.

Personal Career-Ownership Scorecard

Role:
Description – Position Objective
Leadership/Competency Goals – Skills to Be Learned, Mastered, and/or Acquired

---

Activities – Learning Opportunities

Resources – What Is Needed to Be Successful

HAVE FUN

Sounds simple, and it is. This is a great opportunity to reinvent yourself as a professional and grow as a person. If you follow some of the tips I've shared, it should lead you to a job that enhances your experience and engagement in the workplace. Don't get me wrong ... you will still have some challenging days. There's no way to avoid those, even if you work for yourself, but the good will definitely outweigh the bad.

I am glad that I made my decisions to move on. I finally feel like I am in a place where I can continue to thrive and grow. That being said, I know a lot of that has to do with the successes and scars I have gained while I was with my previous employers. Though I wish things could have ended differently with those employers, I'm happy that they led me to where I am today.

Now, I can be a better me, for me and my current employer. Now, I know how to better drive my own career. Now, I have a better understanding of my contributions, and I'm no longer afraid to move on if a company can't nurture and recognize those gifts. Now, I have ***elevated*** to a stronger, more strategic, and effective version of myself. Elevation is required as you continue to progress and evolve in your career. The current version of you will not be able to appropriately support the next level you are trying to ascend to. You have to always look for ways to get better and "level up."

7

FINAL ADVICE AND THOUGHTS

To all of you out there thinking about breaking up, in the process of breaking up, or starting over after your breakup with a previous employer, I hope my experience assists in making your journey a little less complicated and a little more animated as you continue your professional trek.

Just like love, your career takes work and you have to put in that work every day. It will not maintain itself and *you* have to decide what you will get out of it. *You* get to decide what you will and will not take. *You* get to decide how this ends, and only you can say how you'll get there.

If you need to establish a personal board of directors to support you and hold you accountable to your aspirations, do it. If you need to ask yourself the tough questions about whether you should stay or go, ask them. If you've reached your breaking point and need to start over, make it happen. I write all of this to say that *your* career is in *your* control. You are responsible for understanding and mapping out your journey. As you continue to E.V.O.L.V.E., you will put yourself in the best position to completely own your career.

ACKNOWLEDGMENTS

To God be the glory for all the things He has done. I often wondered if this book was going to see the light of day. As you can see, God had plans for me and this book. I thank Him with all of me. His timing is perfect; His ways are right.

To Ernest and Nadine Lee, Daddy and Mommy. It is hard to find the words to express my gratitude to you. When it comes to being parents, you are second to none. When it comes to human beings, you are the best I know. Thank you for raising me so well. Thank you for your love, prayers, sacrifices, chastisement, guidance, and encouragement. Thanks for listening and supporting me when this book was merely a concept. Thanks for reading the book and giving me feedback. Thanks for being my parents. I love you both so much.

To the best siblings ever: Alicia, Erica, and William Lee. As the baby, you all really nurtured, protected, and prepared me for this experience called life in a way only siblings could do. **Alicia**, my Kaybee, you are one of the most selfless people I know and I benefited greatly from that. You spoiled me the most. I truly appreciate how our sisterhood has grown. Thanks for all of our talks, spiritual and natural, and how you have always been a listening ear for me. **Erica**, my E, no matter what or when, I know I can come to you. You are my reality check. Thanks for providing me with a safe space. **William**, Brudder, we've always had a special bond as the youngest two in the family. I knew I could always count on you for anything.

You were always sensible in your guidance and protective in your actions. I love you all, individually and collectively.

To my aunts, uncles, and cousins. Special thanks to the Lees, Williams, Kirkseys, Westfields, and Surratts. Love you all.

To the best publishing team, Silver Tree Publishing. I knew it was meant to be from our very first exchange. The level of dedication, energy, intellect, and drive on this team is remarkable. You all challenged me to dig deeper, think broader, and enthusiastically and genuinely championed me along the way. You all have moved beyond being my publishing team, to being part of my extended family. Thank you to Kate Colbert, Penny Tate, Courtney Hudson, Stephanie Feger, and Sarah Campos for giving your all on my project.

To my editorial board. Your contributions were beyond helpful and reassured me that I was embarking on a necessary and meaningful journey with this book. **Chris Hazen**, since I showed up as your HR Business Partner in Spring, Texas, you have been pushing me to be better and pouring your wisdom into me. You have always been extremely helpful as I've gone through the peaks and valleys of my career. I can't thank you enough for your continuous support. **Roxanne "Roxy" Williams**, I knew I had to get your insight for this book. Your ability to objectively and thoroughly evaluate or create solutions is a true gift. You make it happen as a wife, mother, HR Business Partner, continuous learner, and friend and I'm inspired by how well you manage all these roles. I salute you! **Vaughn Hovey**, professor extraordinaire, I knew before I left your world-class Supply Management Class that I had to stay connected with you. What a wealth of knowledge you are. I've always appreciated how you created an inclusive space for other functions and ideas in your class. You truly showed your commitment to my success and I'm forever grateful. Thank you for your counsel, for every HR hot-topic article with your insights that you've sent me over the years, for helping me find a publisher, and for always making time when I write, call, or ask to meet up. You have gone above and beyond and I'm so thankful to have you as a mentor. **Xavier Smith**, first of all, I'm so proud of you and the career you have established. I admire your dedication to improving the community with your volunteerism. Continue to fearlessly build on the foundation you have created and remember you aren't coming to the table empty handed. You belong. #Period

To Chantell Cargille. Friend, I just have to say how thankful I am to have you in my life. You have been there through some of the best and worst times, always uplifting me, holding me accountable, and believing in me. When I told you about this book you immediately threw your support behind it to help me bring it to life. I can't thank you enough!

To Andrea Stroud. Sister, you are simply amazing. The love and support you have shown to me in life and with this process is indescribable. You were always there to listen to my concepts and ask the questions I'd forget to ask. You challenged and cheered me on at the same time and I can't thank you enough.

To my Sister Tribe: Jill Tidwell, Dr. Tanisha Jackson, Mena Frazier, Mama "Naomi" Stroud, Miquela Moore-Wright, Melissa Devore, and Julia Watson. Thank you for your prayers, support, and pushing me to level up. You all are phenomenal women in your own right and you inspire me to do better. Thank you!

To Mr. Paul and Brenda Bob. Thanks for embracing me as one of your own. I'm proud to be one of your bonus kids. Houston felt more like home because of you two. Thank you for your guidance and love.

To Lanier Robertson, my Shero. You have been my HR proto-type. Thanks for teaching me how to tap into my "softer side" and strategically influence while ensuring I garnered respect. Thanks for handling and developing me with care. I appreciate your continued support.

To Seth Hoffman. Over the years, you have grown from being my friend to becoming my family. You are my brother. I'm so proud of the person and professional you've grown to be. Thanks for listening to all my stories, leveraging Google Translate to try to talk in German and Korean with me (LOL), and being there for me. Thanks for all of your support, Ahjussi!

To my homies: Carlos Washington, Devon Garrett, and Chris Toler. Thanks for allowing me to pick your brains on life, love, and work. Your friendship and support are greatly appreciated.

To my business partners, past and present: Luis Fernandez, Andrew Carroll, Laurie Miller, Bill Brengel, and Christine Camsuzou. Thanks for trusting me to help create and fulfill the vision for your teams. I've learned so much about the chemical industry, and business in general, from you all. The HR function is not always given a seat at the table, but you all truly embraced and leveraged me as a member of your team. Having had the experience of being isolated and only included as a last resort, it's important for me to express how much it means that you welcomed me to bring my authentic self and ideas to our spirited conversations. Thanks for being true leaders and including me in your journeys.

To Daniel LaBelle Photography. Wow ... you did a phenomenal job on my photoshoot for this book and for my website. You went above and beyond for me — from making yourself available on short notice to capturing my best angles. I felt free, confident, and in control, and you provided that environment. Thank you!

To Cara Silletto. I've told you privately but I must reiterate it publicly — I'm so thankful for your support. You willingly agreed to write the foreword for my book and gave me additional insight on strengthen my message. I appreciate the gift and expertise you have shared with me and the rest of world.

To my launch team. THEE Best Launch Team in the world.
I don't know where I would be without your support. You all are very special people in my life and have gone out of your way to dedicate your time, talent, and treasure to making my dream come true and getting this message out. You believed in me and you believed in the message, and I can't thank you enough. This success is every bit yours as it is mine. You have lived this journey with me — whether you were there from birth or a month ago, thanks for pushing me to be better and supporting what God is birthing through me. I love y'all!!!

To my endorsers. You are all phenomenal in your own right. I admire what you do and how you lead. Thank you for inspiring me and supporting my mission to help others E.V.O.L.V.E.

To Al Troiani. The best guitar instructor EVER. You have not only taught me about the guitar, you've taught me about better ways of teaching others. You met me where I was, a complete beginner, and elevated me. When I didn't believe in my ability, you did and made sure I knew it. You encouraged and empowered me. Because of you, I actually wrote the music sheet to "The Break Up Song." It wasn't completely right, LOL, but you cheered me on and helped me fix it. My guitar lessons have been a place of growth and sanctuary for me. You have brought me a long way in six months and I can't thank you enough.

To Al Torrence. Thanks for helping me bring The Break Up Song to life and making my first studio time be a memorable experience. From seeing my vision, working together to build a beautiful track, and bringing out my best vocal performance, you taught and supported me in a way I will never forget. I definitely hope to work with you again. You are doing great things with Music Garden Studios and I wish you continuous success as you help people grow their music.

ABOUT THE AUTHOR

Marissa Lee is a global leader in the Human Resources Business Partner and Workforce Experience space. For the past 10 years, she has combined her passion for people and processes to provide strategic business solutions to Fortune 500 companies in the fashion and chemical industries. She has worked as a business partner in manufacturing, corporate, and distribution-center environments, while gaining both domestic and international experience.

Marissa graduated from The Ohio State University with a Bachelor's degree in business administration with a focus on human resources, logistics, and operations management. In her free time, Marissa is a songwriter, and enjoys spending time with her family and friends. She is also the proud fur-parent to a German-American Rottweiler named Domino Boss.

KEEP IN TOUCH!

🌐 **Learn more about the book, and quickly link to all the social medial channels:**

WhyIBrokeUpWithMyCompany.com

✉ **Send an email:**

Marissa@IAmMarissaLee.com

@ **Find, follow and share on social media:**

Facebook.com/ImMarissaLee
Instagram.com/IAMMarissaLee
LinkedIn.com/in/-IAmMarissaLee

🚀 GO BEYOND THE BOOK ...

Hire Marissa to:

- Deliver a keynote or workshop experience on the *Why I Broke Up with My Company* concept or the E.V.O.L.V.E. career-ownership model

- Facilitate/train teams on developing an employee experience/retention strategy

- Provide guidance on career ownership

- Give career talks

Break Up or Make Up. Continue the conversation by emailing Marissa at Marissa@IAmMarissaLee.com.

Made in the USA
Middletown, DE
16 September 2019